THE AMAZING HUMAN BODY

SKELETAL SYSTEM

KAREN HAYWOOD

mc Marshall Cavendish
Benchmark

Marshall Cavendish Benchmark
99 White Plains Road
Tarrytown, New York 10591
www.marshallcavendish.us

Text copyright © 2009 by Marshall Cavendish Corporation
Illustration on p. 10 by Robert Romagnoli

Editor: Karen Ang
Publisher: Michelle Bisson
Art Director: Anahid Hamparian
Series Designer: Kay Petronio

Library of Congress Cataloging-in-Publication Data
Haywood, Karen.
Skeletal system / by Karen Haywood.
p. cm. — (The amazing human body)
Includes bibliographical references and index.
Summary: "Discusses the parts that make up the human skeletal system, what can go wrong, how to treat those illnesses and diseases, and how to stay healthy"—Provided by publisher.
ISBN 978-0-7614-3056-8
1. Human skeleton—Juvenile literature. I. Title. II. Series.
QM101.H42 2009
611—dc22
2008017574

 = bone matrix

Front cover: The human skeletal system
Back Cover: The knee
Photo research by Tracey Engel
Front cover photo: Brand X/Shutterstock
The photographs in this book are used by permission and through the courtesy of:
Alamy: Phototake Inc., 4, 31, 35, 40, 49, 52; Elvele Images, 16; Scott Camazine, 23, 39; MedicalRF.com, 28; Michael Diggin, 36, back cover; Medical-on-Line, 57; The Stock Asylum, LLC, 64; Photo Researchers, Inc.: 9, Science Source, 7, SPL, 8; BSIP, 17; Steve Gschmeissner, 21 (middle), 22; Eye of Science, 21 (bottom); John M. Daugherty, 24; Gustoimages, 26; D. Roberts, 29 (top), 29 (bottom); Dave Roberts, 30; Zephyr, 44, 46 (bottom), 56; Du Cane Medical Imaging Ltd., 46 (top); CNRI, 54; Aaron Haupt, 58; Gary Carlson, 60; Phanie, 63; Shutterstock: Sebastian Kaulitzki, 12, 42 ; Sonya Etchison, 38; topal, 43; trialart-info, 48; Tihis, 52; Margit, 66; Sally Scott, 69; PhotoCreate, 70; Polina Lobanova, 71; SuperStock: Image Source Black, 14, 41; Custom Medical Stock Photo: L. Birmingham, 19; Phototake: ISM, 21 (top); Corbis: Mediscan, 61.
Printed in China
123456

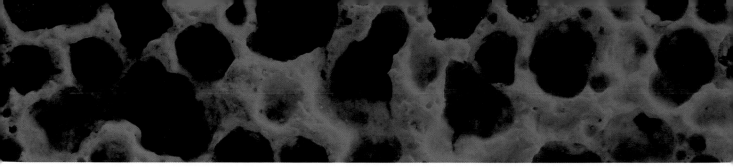

CONTENTS

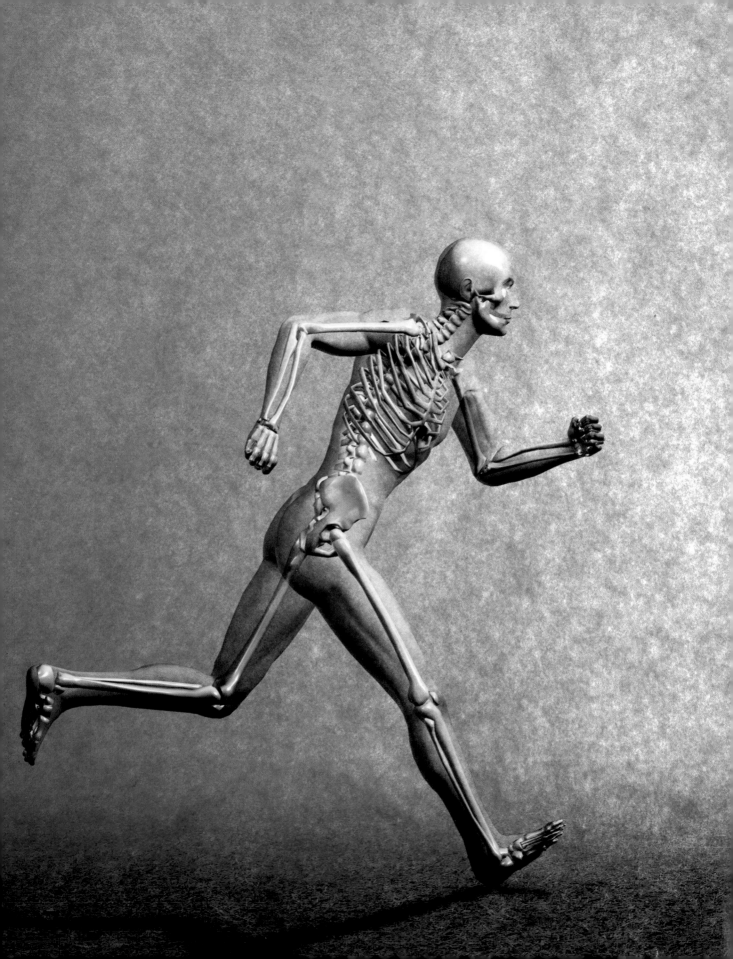

1

What Is the Skeletal System?

The skeletal system—also called the skeleton—weighs only about 20 pounds (9 kilograms) in human adults, but is made up of 206 bones. Bones differ in size, shape, weight, and in some cases, what they are made of. This variety is due to the different functions of the skeleton: to provide the framework and support of the body, protect the tissues and organs in the body cavities, act as levers for muscle action, and provide a site for blood cell production.

Without your skeletal system, you would not be able to walk, run, or even stand up.

THE STUDY OF BONES

The study of bones, or osteology, goes back thousands of years. The ancient Egyptians wrote about medical treatments for bones, and other parts of the body, as far back as 3000 BCE. Around 400 BCE, Hippocrates, a famous Greek physician, wrote extensively about dislocated and broken bones, which he treated with bandages and splints.

The word skeleton comes from the Greek *skeletos*, which means dried up or withered. This name is actually a bit of a misnomer since bones are one-third water and made of living tissue that can grow and change. When they used *skeletos*, the ancient Greeks were actually referring to a mummy or to very old skeletal remains.

Scientists from different parts of the world studied bones and furthered scientific knowledge of the human body. In the second century CE the Greco-Roman physician and teacher Claudius Galen of Pergamon—commonly referred to as Galen—taught the importance of studying osteology. Abd al-Latif al-Baghdadi, an Arab scholar who lived from 1162 to 1231, was familiar with the work of Galen and expanded on it. In the fifteenth century, Leonardo da Vinci studied the human skeleton in great detail based on thorough dissections of the body. In order to make his drawings more accurate, he observed how the bones functioned with the muscles to produce movements. In the mid-sixteenth century, a Flemish scholar, Andreas Vesalius, wrote *De Humani Corporis Fabrica*—On the Fabric of the Human Body—which is now considered to be groundbreaking work in the study of human anatomy.

At the University of Paris in 1741, Nicholas Andry coined the term orthopedics from the Greek *orthos* (straight) and *paidion* (young child). His focus was to teach methods of preventing and correcting bone disorders in children. John Hunter, a British surgeon who lived in the 1700s, discovered that bones are living tissue that can change. He showed how bones grow

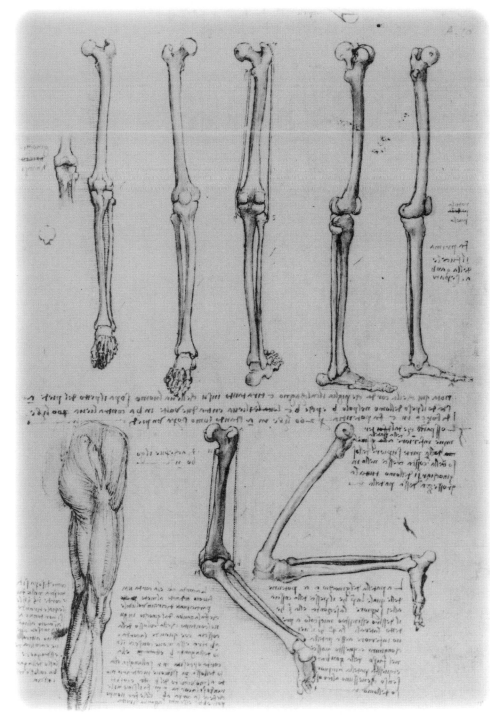

These illustrations of bones were drawn by Leonardo da Vinci nearly six hundred years ago.

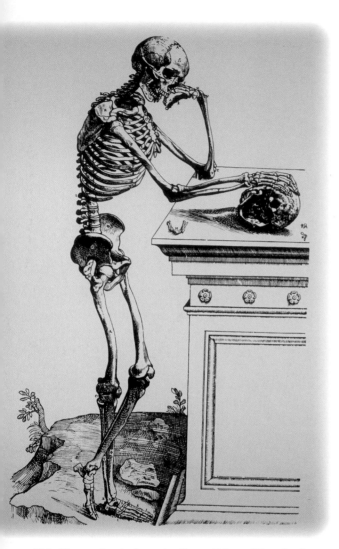

This illustration is from the first edition of Vesalius's De Humani Corporis Fabrica.

by the continuous remodeling of layers. In 1817, Robert Chesser devoted most of his time to treating bone fractures and deformities and creating splints and other medical equipment.

However, Jean-Andre Venel—who lived from 1740 to 1791—is often considered the true father of orthopedics. Venel was a physician who established the world's first orthopedic institute in the Swiss town of Orbe. This was the first hospital that dealt specifically with the treatment for skeletal deformities in crippled children. Venel recorded and published all his methods, and became known as the first true orthopedist.

Hugh Owen Thomas is remembered in history as the grandfather of British orthopedic surgery. In the 1800s he made splints that kept the limbs of patients with inflamed joints—the parts where two bones meet—motionless while allowing them to walk. The Thomas Splint was introduced to the battlefields of World War I by his nephew, Sir Robert Jones. This splint helped decrease the death rate for people who had serious fractures in the femur—the long bone found in the thigh. In 1916, the death rate was 80 percent, but by 1918 it dropped to just 8 percent. Robert Jones also invented an osteoclast to break and reset deformed bones, as well as a collar for bone problems in the neck.

The discovery of X rays in 1895, by the German physicist Wilhelm Conrad Röntgen, led to a revolution in the science of osteology, orthopedics, and the treatment of skeletal disorders. With X rays, the outlines of the bones can be seen through the skin and muscle covering them, allowing the physician to better see fractures, injuries, or deformities.

From the twentieth century into the twenty-first, advances in medical science moved more quickly than ever before in history, with new innovations seeming to occur overnight. Scientists and doctors have found efficient ways to treat and prevent diseases associated with bones. Bone cells have been closely examined and are now used to treat diseases that affected other parts of the body, such as leukemia.

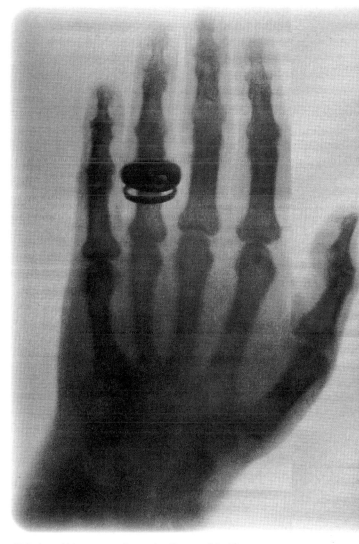

This hand X ray was from the first public X ray demonstration by Röntgen. It shows the bones of the hand and the ring that the man was wearing.

The future in bone research looks very bright. But none of this would be possible without the discoveries of those early physicians and osteologists. Thanks to them, we now know a lot about the human skeletal system.

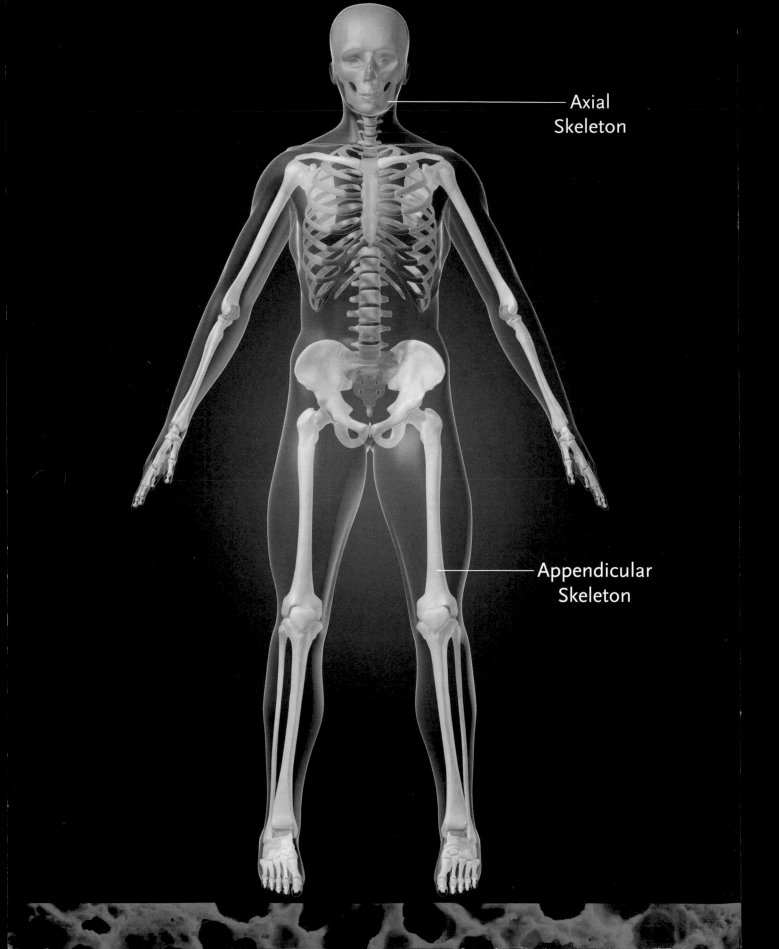

Axial
Skeleton

Appendicular
Skeleton

OVERVIEW OF THE HUMAN SKELETON

But what are these 206 bones that hold you upright and protect your vital organs? The adult human skeleton is divided into two main groups of bones—the axial skeleton and the appendicular skeleton.

The Axial Skeleton

The first structure of the axial skeleton is the skull, which is the bony framework of the head. The skull houses the brain and many sensory organs. The two main areas of the skull are the cranium and the face. The skull contains twenty-two bones, many of which are paired. The face contains fourteen bones. The lower jaw bone, called the mandible, is the skull's only moveable bone and the only one not directly connected to the other bones of the skull.

In an adult, the skull and the upper body are supported by the twenty-six bones of the vertebral column. (Each of the twenty-six bones is called a vertebra.) The vertebral column—or spine—runs along the back of the body and connects to the bones of the chest, or thorax. In front, the thorax has a three-part bone called the sternum—or breastbone—and twelve pairs of ribs. The ribs connect the sternum to the vertebral column.

The Appendicular Skeleton

The upper portion of the appendicular skeleton is composed of the pectoral, or shoulder, girdle and the arm bones. The pectoral girdle consists of two bones—the collarbone, also called the clavicle, in the front, and a flat, triangular bone called the scapula, or shoulder blade, at the back of the body.

Articulating—or connecting at a joint—with the pectoral girdle is the upper arm bone called the humerus. The two lower arm bones, the radius and the ulna, connect with the humerus at the elbow. The wrist contains

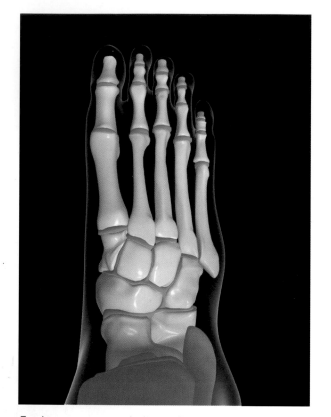

Toe bones are very similar to finger bones. They are all called phalanges.

eight small carpal bones arranged in two rows of four. Five metacarpal bones form the framework for the palm of each hand. Each finger bone is called a phalanx. There are fourteen phalanges (plural for phalanx) in each hand—two for the thumb and three for each finger.

The lower portion of the appendicular skeleton is composed of the pelvic girdle and the leg bones. The pelvis, or hip bone, appears to be just one bone, but it is actually composed of three bones called the ilium, ischium, and pubis. The lower extremities—the legs—connect to the pelvic girdle at the acetabulum socket. Each leg is formed by the femur (thigh bone), the patella (kneecap), and the two lower leg bones, the tibia (shin bone) and the fibula. The structure of the foot is similar to the hand, but it is much stronger. The ankle contains seven tarsal bones and the foot has five metatarsals. Like fingers, the toes contain fourteen phalanges.

ANATOMICAL DIRECTIONS IN THE BODY

Doctors, scientists, and other professionals often use scientific terms to describe parts or actions in the body. The following chart will help you to better understand the location and movement of bones in the skeleton.

ASPECT, OR POSITION	DEFINITION
Superior	Above or in a higher position; toward the head
Inferior	Below or in a lower position; toward the feet
Ventral or Anterior	Located in or toward the front of the body
Dorsal or Posterior	Located in or toward the back of the body
Cranial	Closer to the head
Caudal	Closer to the pelvis
Medial	Toward the navel
Lateral	Toward the side, farther away from the navel
Proximal	Closer to the origin of a structure
Distal	Farther from the origin of a structure
Prone	Body lying on the stomach with the face downward
Supine	Body lying on the back with the face upward

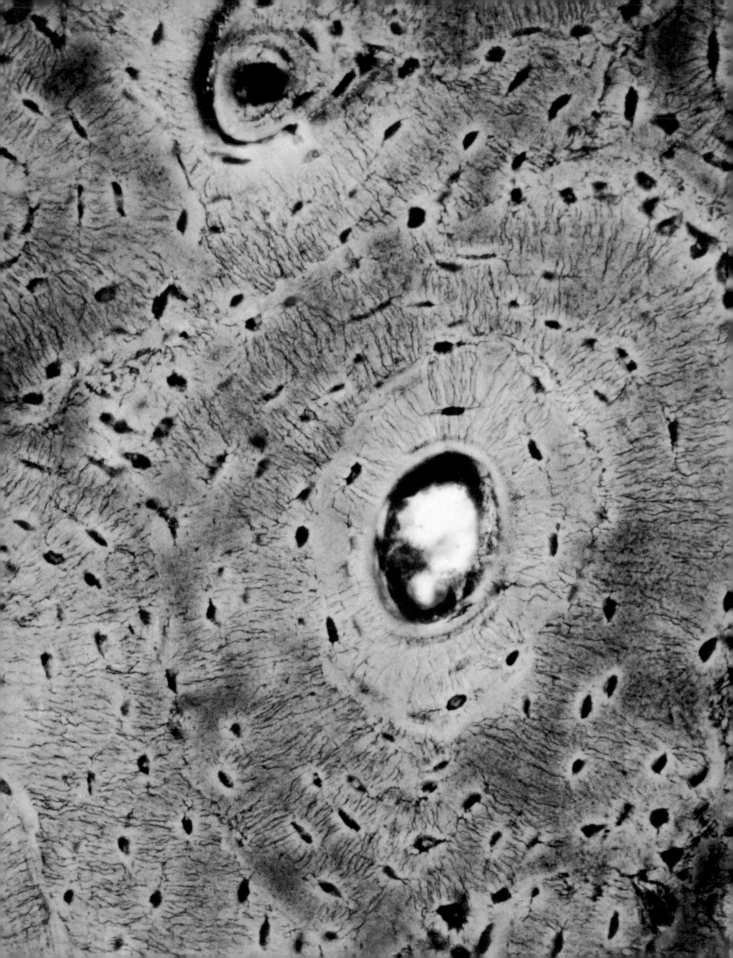

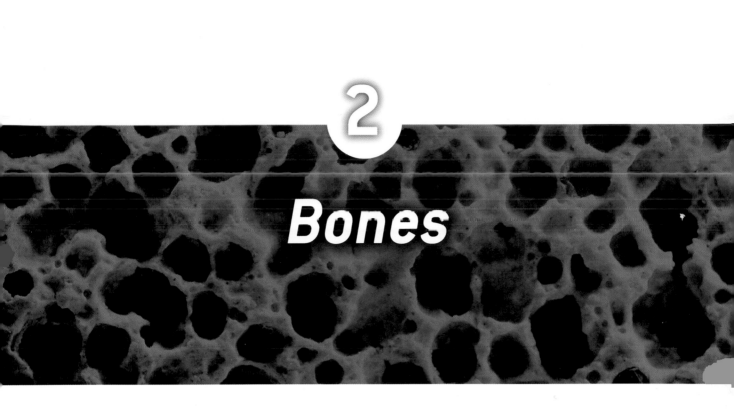

2

Bones

Bones make up the skeletal system. They come in different shapes and sizes. Some come in pairs or sets. Bones may connect to each other, sit on top of one another, and some are even fused together to form a larger structure.

Each bone is made up of many different parts. Various cells within the bone have specific jobs that help to make the bone healthy and strong.

Human bones are made of many different substances arranged in ways that make bones strong.

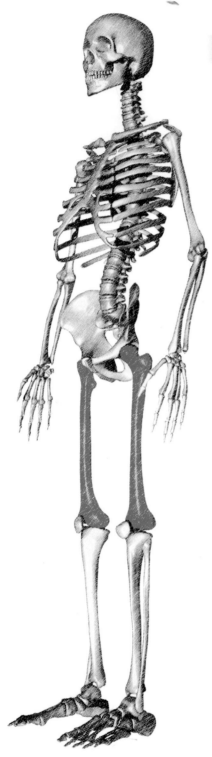

Located in the thighs, the femurs (green) are the longest bones in the body.

WHAT DOES A BONE LOOK LIKE?

A bone's shape determines how much movement is possible at a particular joint. There are flat bones, long bones, short bones, sesamoid (rounded) bones, and irregular bones.

Bones of the skull, the scapula, sternum, and the ribs are examples of flat bone. These bones may be flat in design to provide a surface for muscle or they may be flat in order to provide protection.

The shape of a long bone is familiar to most people. A long bone's length exceeds its thickness. It has a long narrow shaft—called the diaphysis—and two irregular ends, each called an epiphysis. Long bones are designed to function as a lever and are used for movement. For example, in the leg the femur acts as an attachment point for the muscles. As the muscles contract, they cause the femur to move at the hip. Other long bones include the clavicle, humerus, radius, ulna, tibia, and fibula, and also the metacarpals, metatarsals, and phalanges.

The short bone tends to resemble a cube, and is found in the wrists and ankles as carpals and tarsals. Short bones connect with many other bones and transfer the flow of movement from bone to bone.

A sesamoid bone, a type of short bone, occurs mainly in the hands and feet. However, the patella, or kneecap, is also a sesamoid bone. Sesamoid bones are usually embedded within a tendon or within a joint capsule.

Irregular bones make up the vertebral column. Other irregular bones include the hyoid bone and the sacrum. They fall under the irregular category mainly because they fit in no other.

Some bones have projections, or parts that stick out. Most bones have distinctive features called bone markings. These markings include pits, grooves, and depressions that help form joints or serve as spots for muscle attachment. Bones also have holes that allow nerves and blood vessels to pass through.

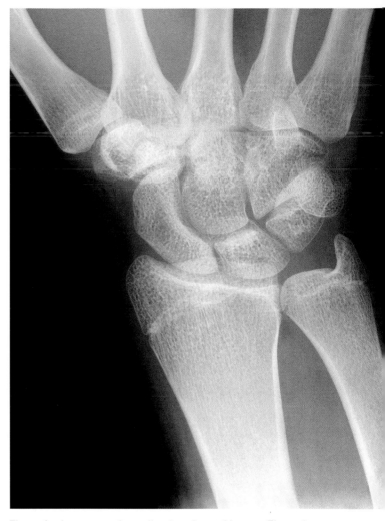

The wrist has several small cube-shaped bones. These bones make the wrist flexible and capable of different types of movement.

WHAT ARE BONES MADE OF?

Bones are not empty and lifeless—they are dynamic, living organs. Although the spaces between the living cells of bone tissue are filled with organic salts—such as calcium carbonate (7 percent) and calcium phosphate (85 percent) and small amounts of sodium and magnesium—

BONE PARTS

PROJECTIONS	
head	a rounded, knoblike end connected to the rest of the bone by a slender region of the bone called the neck
process	a large projection of a bone, such as the upper part of the ulna that creates the elbow (also known as the olecranon process)
crest	a distinct border or ridge—often rough—such as the iliac crest over the top of the hip bone (this crest is an attachment point for ligaments and muscles of the abdomen and leg)
spine	a sharp projection from the surface of a bone, such as the spine of the shoulder blade (scapula)

DEPRESSIONS OR HOLES	
foramen (plural is *foramina*)	a hole that allows a vessel or a nerve to pass through or between bones, such as the jugular foramen, which allows passage of the internal jugular vein (the vein that drains blood from the brain)
sinus	a space found in some skull bones that provide an area for air to collect
fossa (plural is *fossae*)	a depression on a bone surface, such as the mandibular fossa where the jawbone joins with the face
meatus	a short channel or passageway, such as the channel in the temporal bone of the skull that leads to the inner ear

the bone cells themselves are very much alive. Bone is made of living cells along with large amounts of ground substances, which is also called matrix. The matrix is about 20 percent water, 20 percent protein, and 60 percent mineral salts. Bones also have their own system of blood vessels, lymphatic vessels (a part of the immune system), and nerves.

There are two types of bone—or osseous—tissue, and their names refer to how they differ in density, or how tightly the tissue is packed together. One type is compact bone, which is hard and dense. Compact bone forms the outer shells of all bone and also the shafts in long bones. The cells in this type of bone are located in rings of matrix around a central canal. This Haversian canal contains nerves and blood vessels.

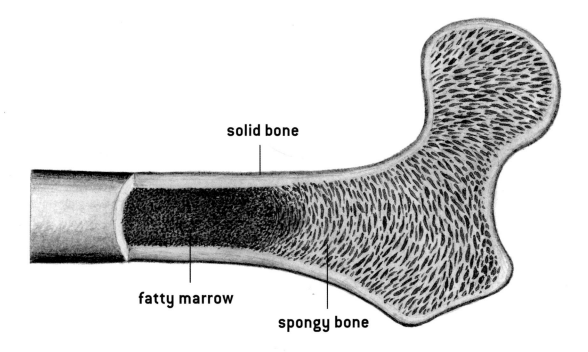

solid bone

fatty marrow

spongy bone

Different types of bone—found within the same bone—are perfectly designed to do their jobs. Having too much of one kind of bone would make your bones weaker and less efficient.

The second type of bone, called spongy bone, is found at the ends of long bones. It is lighter and less dense than compact bone. The spongy bone of the femur, humerus, and sternum consists of struts and plates (trabeculae) and bars of bone. These trabeculae and bars are next to small, unevenly shaped cavities that contain red bone marrow. The red marrow within the spongy bone of the femoral epiphysis (the end of the femur) is an important site for blood cell formation. Also, spongy bone reduces the weight of the skeleton and makes it easier for muscles to move the bones.

Bone Cells

There are three types of bone cells based on form (their structure), function (what they do), and location (where they are): osteoblasts, osteocytes, and osteoclasts. These bone cells perform five functions

- produce the protein in bone

- promote the mineralization of the protein matrix

- maintain the bone tissues

- control bone resorption, or the breaking down of bone and the release of minerals into the blood

- play an active role in mineral physiology.

When a fetus (a developing human inside its mother's womb) is about two to three months old, bone formation, or ossification, begins. At this time, osteoblasts, the bone-producing cells, become active and begin to manufacture the protein matrix called osteoid. This substance contains large amounts of collagen, a fibrous protein that gives strength and flexibility to the tissue. With the help of enzymes, calcium compounds are deposited within the matrix. This mineralization—or hardening—occurs over a period of months. Once the osteoblasts harden around the cells, they are known as osteocytes.

Osteocytes are mature bone cells that maintain bone structure in adults. They are smaller and less active than osteoblasts, and are housed in a small chamber called a lacuna—a small cavity—contained in the hardened matrix of bone. Osteocytes were once thought to be inactive cells. However, there is now evidence that they can produce collagen and control bone mineralization within their lacunae (which is the plural for lacuna).

The third type of bone cell is the osteoclast, which is involved in bone resorption, or breaking down bone. This cell actively reabsorbs old or fatigued bone so that new bone may be replaced by osteoblast cells. This resorption is necessary for remodeling of bone during growth, and repair. A balance between osteoblasts and osteoclasts maintains bone tissue. When osteoclast cells reabsorb bone faster than the osteoblast cells can build it, osteoporosis, or bone loss, occurs.

Bone Marrow

The central marrow cavity of a long bone is called the medullary cavity. The space within this cavity is filled with a particular type of soft connective tissue called bone marrow. Bones contain two kinds of marrow, both of which are made up mainly of blood cells and fat cells. Red marrow is found at the ends of the long bones and at the centers of other bones. Stem cells reproduce inside

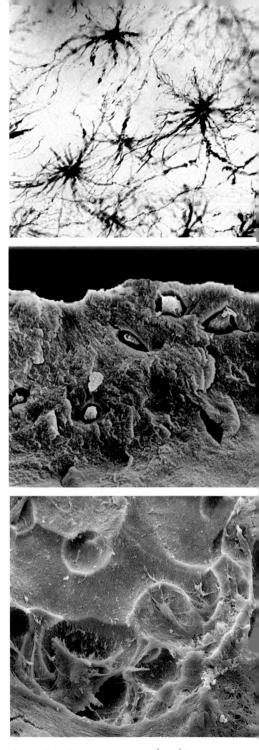

Bone-forming osteoblasts (top) harden to become osteocytes (middle), which are embedded within bones. Osteoclasts (bottom; shown in green) break down old or damaged bone cells. Bone can then be rebuilt by osteoblasts, and the process begins again.

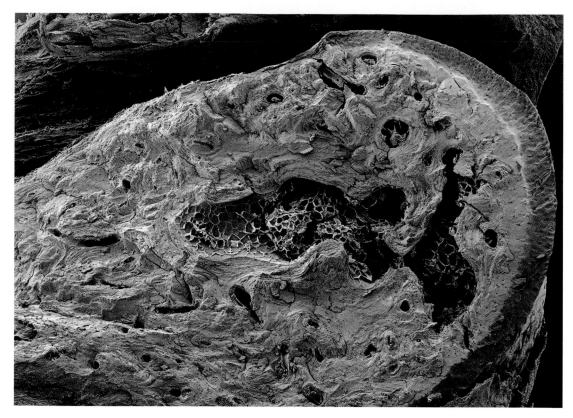

The red bone marrow found inside the bones is essential for healthy blood cell development.

red bone marrow. These special cells form the cellular components of the blood and immune system. Red marrow is more commonly found in young people. Yellow marrow is found chiefly in the central cavities of the long bones, is composed largely of fat, and is found in the bones of adults. This type of marrow can be used to produce more blood cells.

Bone Membranes

The diaphysis area of long bones, and most of all other bones, is covered on the outside— except at the joint—by a membrane called the periosteum. The inner layer of this membrane contains osteoblasts that are essential to growth, development, and repair of bone. The blood vessels and lymphatic vessels of the periosteum play a vital role in the nourishment of bone tissue. The membrane also has nerves that send messages to your brain. When bone fractures occur, the pain is carried to the brain by nerves running through the periosteum. A thinner membrane, the endosteum, lines the marrow cavity of a bone. The endosteum also contains cells related to bone development and breakdown.

THE JOINTS

A joint—or articulation, as it is also called—is an area where two or more bones come together. Joints hold the bones of the skeletal system together while giving the skeleton mobility. Because bones are rigid, movement can occur only where two bones articulate, or meet together as joints.

Joints can have different purposes. For example, in the skull, a joint may serve to resist force placed upon it so that those bones do not move. At the shoulder or hip, a joint may be an essential factor in movement. There are several ways of classifying joints. One method is based on the type of material found between the bones.

The bones in a fibrous joint are held together by fibrous connective tissue. These joints are found only at the sutures between the bones of the skull. This type of articulation is immovable and is called a synarthrosis.

Cartilaginous joints connect bones by using cartilage. Examples are the joints between the parts of the spine, or

Unlike other joints, the joints in the skull—seen here as faint lines—are not supposed to move.

backbone, and between the pubic bones of the pelvis—the pubic symphysis. This type of articulation permits a slight degree of movement and is called an amphiarthrosis.

The bones in synovial joints are held together by ligaments, which are bands of fibrous connective tissue. Ligaments reinforce and help stabilize articulations at various points. Synovial joints may also contain other structural components to aid in function, including tendons, tendon sheaths, bursae, menisci, and fat pads. A synovial joint is freely movable and is called a diarthrosis (plural form is diarthroses). Most joints are synovial joints.

Bones connected by synovial joints have a narrow space between them called the joint cavity. This cavity contains a small amount of thick, colorless fluid that helps to prevent friction, heat, and deterioration within the joint. This lubricant, synovial fluid, looks similar to uncooked egg whites and is produced by the membrane that lines the joint cavity. It lubricates the joint, nourishes the cells in the area of the articulation, and absorbs shocks.

Joints can be lubricated either by "weeping lubrication," in which the synovial fluid absorbed by the cartilage is pressed out when the articulated surfaces touch. Lubrication can also occur through "boosted lubrication," which happens when the articular cartilage absorbs some molecules of the synovial fluid, allowing small compounds to remain behind and lubricate the joint.

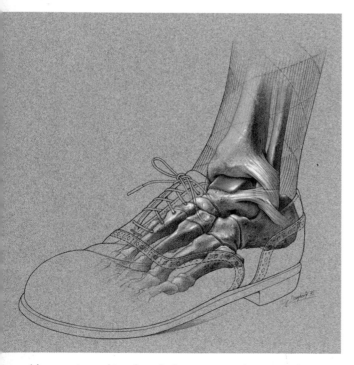

Ligaments and tendons help to connect bones and form joints, allowing movement.

TYPES OF SYNOVIAL JOINTS

The chart below lists the six types of synovial joints or diarthroses.

DIARTHROSIS	SHAPE AND MOVEMENT	EXAMPLE
condyloid or ellipsoid	Convex to concave in shape. Allows movement in two directions	Between metacarpal and first phalanx of finger
ball and socket	Ball fitting into cup-like depression. Gives greatest freedom of movement	Shoulder Hip
gliding	Flat or slightly curved. Bones' surfaces slide over one another.	Wrist Ankle
saddle	One bone shaped like a saddle, the other bone fits into it, similar to condyloid with deeper surfaces. Allows the thumb to touch the tips of the other fingers.	Carpal to metacarpal; wrist to thumb
pivot	Round. Allows rotation	Between first and second cervical (neck) vertebrae. (Allows head to move from side to side.)
hinge	Convex to concave in shape.	Elbow Knee

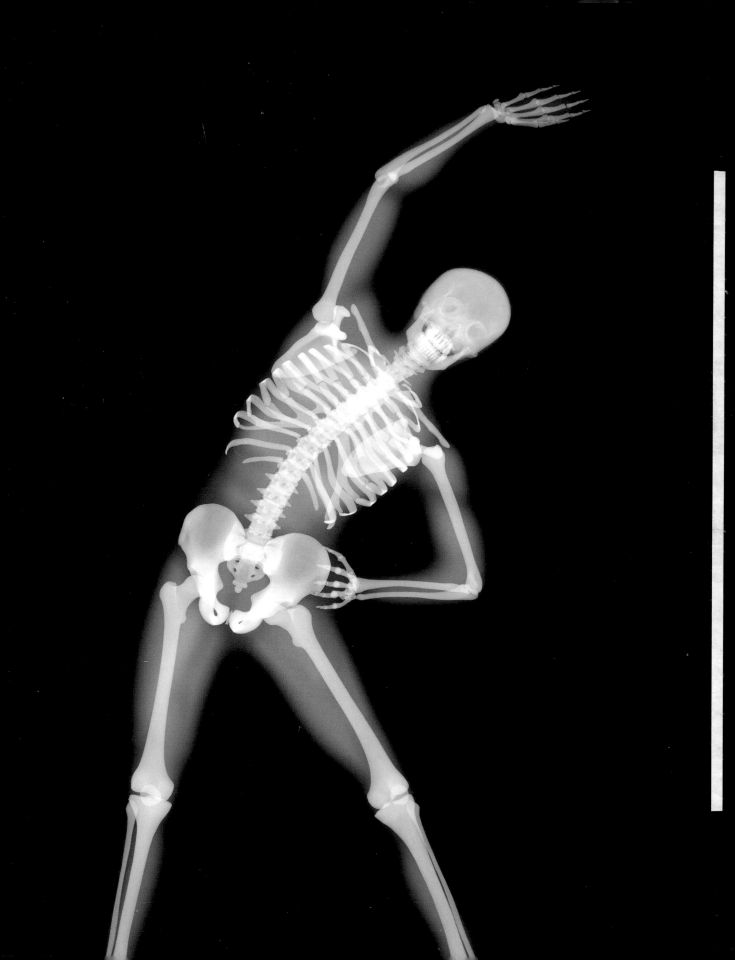

3

Functions of the Skeletal System

What do the 206 bones of the human skeletal system do to help the body function? The role of the bones of the skeletal system can be grouped into five major categories:

- protection
- structural support
- movement
- mineral and chemical warehousing
- blood cell and platelet production

A computer image based on a human X ray shows how the skeletal system is essential to movement.

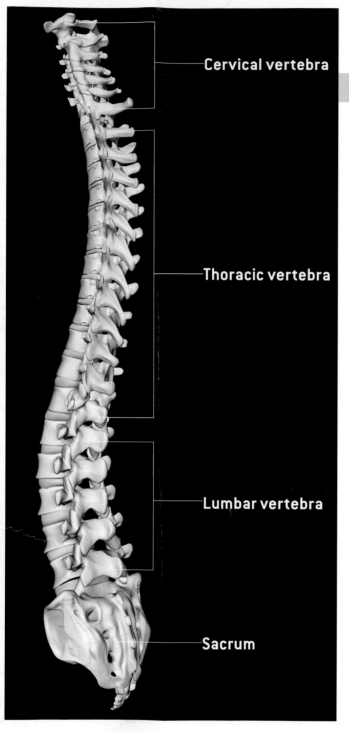

Cervical vertebra

Thoracic vertebra

Lumbar vertebra

Sacrum

The spine, or spinal column, is divided into four different sections. The cervical vertebrae are located in the neck area; the thoracic vertebrae are in the chest or upper back region; and the lumbar vertebrae are along the lower back. The sacrum is a set of fused vertebrae and is located at the bottom of the spine where it connects with the hipbones.

PROTECTION

Bone is one of the strongest materials in nature, making it an ideal material to protect the more vulnerable tissues and organs of the body. In some cases, strong bones can resist pressure even better than some of the best reinforced concrete. Without this protection, vital organs would be more exposed to great harm.

The cranium, or skull, protects the soft and delicate brain, by enclosing it in a rounded chamber. The cranium also houses the ear and forms part of the eye socket. Bones of the skull join with facial bones that protect these sensory organs.

The vertebral, or spinal, column encloses the spinal cord. The spinal cord is part of the central nervous system and allows you to breathe, move, and feel sensations. Connected to the spine are twelve pairs of ribs. These ribs protect the heart, lungs, and other organs. The pelvis is located toward the bottom of the spine and shields organs of the urinary and reproductive systems.

BABY BONES

Bones are especially important to babies and small children as their young organs develop and grow. However, because the bones are not fully developed, they do not provide as much protection as adult bones. An infant's skull has areas where bone formation is not complete. These areas are called soft spots, or fontanels. The largest fontanel is near the front of the skull where the different parts of the skull meet. This soft spot normally does not completely close until the age of 18 months. This is one reason why babies' bodies are so fragile and a lot of internal damage can occur with injuries. A newborn baby may have 150 more bones than its mother, but many of them are composed of cartilage. As the baby grows older, the bones fuse, or grow together, thereby reducing the total number of bones in the skeletal system.

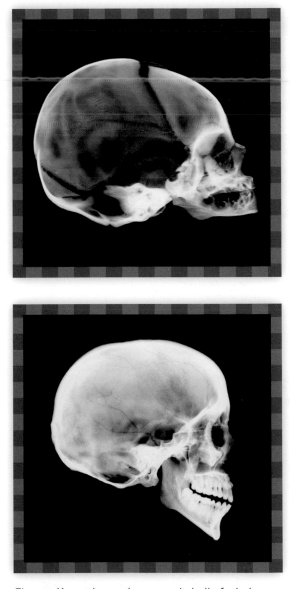

The top X ray shows the normal skull of a baby. The bottom X ray shows an adult human skull that is fully formed and has no soft spots.

STRUCTURAL SUPPORT

The bones of the skeletal system collectively form a supporting framework and give shape to the human body. This framework can bear heavy loads without becoming deformed and also protects and supports vital organs and soft tissues against the force of gravity. The skeleton also provides attachment sites for many muscles. If not for our supporting framework, we would resemble a jellyfish.

The bones also give shape, or form, to the body. Bones of the skull and face, for example, determine the shape of the head. The size and shape of bones are usually associated with the functions they perform. For example, because they can give birth to babies, women have a relatively wider pelvis than men. Another example is the tibia. The shape of the tibia is much like that of a column. Like a column, the tibia is designed to support a great deal of weight.

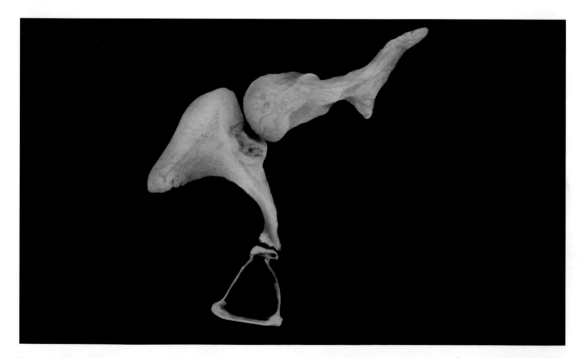

The smallest bones in the body are located in the middle ear. The three middle ear bones—the hammer (upper right), anvil (middle) and stirrup (bottom)—transmit vibrations that help you hear sounds.

The Skeletal System

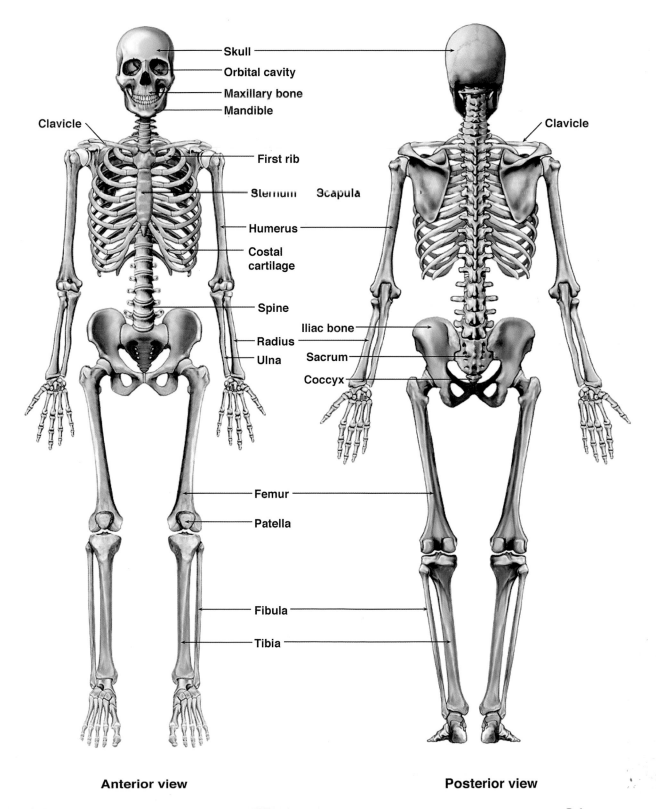

Skull

Orbital cavity

Maxillary bone

Mandible

Clavicle

First rib

Sternum   Scapula

Humerus

Costal cartilage

Spine

Radius

Ulna

Clavicle

Iliac bone

Sacrum

Coccyx

Femur

Patella

Fibula

Tibia

Anterior view

Posterior view

Adult Bones and Their Functions

AREA/REGION	NAME OF BONE	STRUCTURAL FUNCTION
Skull or Cranium (8 bones)	frontal	Forms the forehead, front of the skull's roof, roof of the eye socket.
	parietals (2)	Form most of the top and side walls of the cranium.
	temporal (2)	Form part of the sides and some of the base of skull.
	ethmoid	Located between the eyes. Forms part of eye socket, cranial floor, and most of nasal cavity roof.
	sphenoid	Forms part of eye socket. Holds and protects the pituitary gland (part of the endocrine system).
	occipital	Forms much of the back and lower surfaces of the cranium. The *foramen magnum,* located at the base of the occipital bone, is the large opening through which the spinal cord communicates with the brain.
Facial Bones (14)	mandible	Lower jawbone. Houses teeth.
	maxillae (2)	Upper jawbone and part of hard palate (roof of mouth). Houses teeth.
	zygomatics (2)	Cheekbones
	nasals (2)	Form the bridge of the nose.
	lacrimals (2)	Inside corner of the eye
	vomer	Forms lower part of nasal septum.
	palatines (2)	Form back of hard palate.
	conchae (2)	Inferior nasal conchae form lateral walls of nasal cavity.

AREA/REGION	NAME OF BONE	STRUCTURAL FUNCTION
Ossicles (Ears, 6)	incudes (2)	Middle bone of three in middle ear that transmits acoustic vibrations from eardrum to inner ear—also called the anvil.
	mallei (2)	Ossicle attached to the eardrum—also called the hammer.
	stapedes (2)	Innermost of the three small bones of the middle ear—also called the stirrup.
Throat (1)	hyoid	U-shaped bone below the skull to which the tongue is attached. It is the only bone that is not attached to another bone.
Vertebral Column (26)	cervical (7)	First cervical vertebra is the atlas, which supports the head. Second is the axis, serves as pivot when head is turned.
	thoracic (12)	Located in chest, back ends of the 12 ribs are attached to these vertebrae.
	lumbar (5)	Support heavy weight, located in small of back.
	sacrum (5 fused, or joined together)	Forms back part of bony pelvis.
	coccyx (4 fused)	Tailbone
Thorax (25)	ribs (12 pairs)	Form the chest, the thoracic cage, support pectoral girdles and arms.
	sternum (3 bones fused together as one)	Breastbone, articulates with ribs to support upper body. Sternum has 3 parts: manubrium, body, and xiphoid process
Pectoral or Shoulder Girdle (4)	clavicle (2)	Collarbones; help support shoulder, link scapula to sternum. Most frequently broken bone.
	scapula (2)	Shoulder blades; connect the humerus with the clavicle.
Arms (6)	humerus (2)	Long bone of the upper arm; forms a joint with the scapula and with the radius and ulna at the elbow; deltoid (shoulder) muscle attaches to humerus.
	radius (2)	Long forearm bone that lies on the side above the thumb; articulates with the humerus at the elbow and with carpals at the wrist.

AREA/REGION	NAME OF BONE	STRUCTURAL FUNCTION
	ulna (2)	Longer forearm bone on the side in line with the little finger; articulates with the humerus at the elbow and with carpals at the wrist.
Wrist and Hand (54)	carpals (16)	Bones of the wrist arranged in 2 rows of 4; the proximal row articulates with the radius and ulna, the distal row with the metacarpals; serves as joint allowing hand to move.
	metacarpals (10)	Framework for the palm of each hand
	phalanges (28)	Finger bones: 2 for each thumb, 3 for each finger
Pelvic Girdle (2)	os coxae (2)	Hip bones; each begins as 3 separate bones that later fuse together: ilium, ischium, and pubis. Supports organs in the lower abdomen including urinary bladder, internal reproductive organs, and parts of the intestine. Also supports weight when one sits down.
Legs (8)	femur (2)	Thigh bone; longest and strongest bones in body, articulate with os coxae
	patella (2)	Kneecap; example of sesamoid bone, embedded in tendon of large anterior thigh muscle, covers and protects knee joint; primary function is knee extension; increases leverage the tendon can exert on the femur.
	tibia (2)	Shin bone; long, weight-bearing bone of lower leg; articulates with the femur and patella in superior aspect, the fibula laterally and with the ankle in inferior aspect.
	fibula (2)	Slender bone of lower leg, The fibula supports approximately one-sixth of the body weight and produces the lateral (outer) prominence of the ankle.
Foot and Ankle (52)	tarsals (14)	The ankle; the bones or cartilages between the metatarsus and the leg, consisting of 7 short bones. The calcaneus, the heel bone, is the largest tarsal; it transmits most weight to the ground. The Achilles tendon attaches the calf muscle to the calcaneus.
	metatarsals (10)	The bones that travel out to each toe in the foot; articulate with the tarsals in the hind foot and the phalanges in the forefoot; they form the frame of the instep, and the heads form the ball of the foot.
	phalanges (28)	Toe bones: 2 for each great toe, 3 for each other toes

MOVEMENT

We are able to move because of our body's joints. The structure of each joint, or articulation, is well matched with its function. Some articulations allow a large amount, or a great range, of movement, or joint mobility. Others are built for joint stability and strongly resist movement. The degree of range of motion is governed by how well the joints fit together and by the amount of support provided by the tissues (muscles, tendons, and ligaments) surrounding the joint. The shoulder joint, for example, has quite significant range of motion. This movement is allowed by the rather loose fit of the ball and socket joint between the head of the humerus and the shallow fossa of the scapula. Suture joints of the skull are examples of zero joint mobility, which means they should not move. These articulations are formed by bones that link together like the pieces of a jigsaw puzzle.

The movements of our arms and legs occur at major joints such as the hip, knee, ankle, shoulder, elbow, and wrist, where bones function as mechanical levers. When muscles pull on bone, they create rotational effects at joints. The joints then rotate around an imaginary line called the axis of rotation. Joint mobility can range from very slight movement (think of a guitarist's fingers) to the

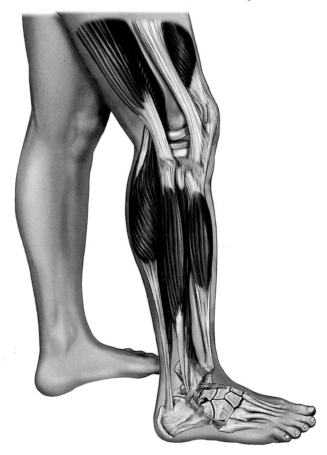

The bones and joints serve as anchoring points for muscles, ligaments and tendons.

complex, multijoint movements of a gymnast, contortionist, or the extraordinary acrobatics of performers in circuses.

Types of Joint Movement

There are four types of joint movement: gliding, angular, rotation, and a category of unique joint mobility called special movements.

Gliding, or sliding, is the simplest type of motion. It involves one surface moving over another without any rotation or angular motion. Gliding motion occurs at the intercarpal (wrist) and intertarsal (ankle) joints.

Angular motion decreases or increases the angle between two adjoining bones when a body part moves. For example, when you bring your forearm

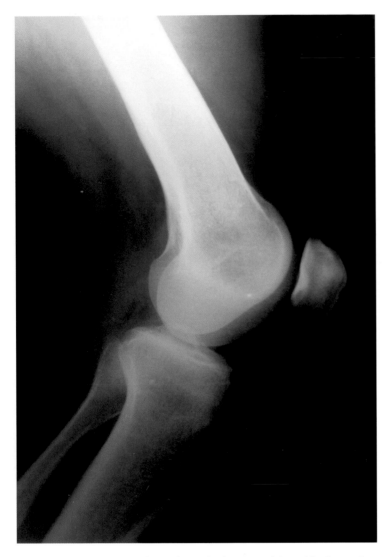

The kneecap, or patella, is a triangular bone positioned in front of the knee. It protects the knee joint.

up to flex the muscles of your bicep, the angle between your forearm and bicep decreases.

Rotational mobility, or rotation, is a joint movement that allows a bone to turn on its own long axis. Rotation occurs at the hip and shoulder. However, the most obvious example of rotation is the head turning right and left, as though you are shaking your head "No!"

Common Types of Angular Motion

ANGULAR MOTION	DESCRIPTION	EXAMPLES OF JOINT WHERE IT CAN OCCUR
Abduction	To move an extremity away from the midline, which is an imaginary vertical line drawn down the center of the body.	Hip (when a leg is lifted out to the side)
Adduction	To move the extremity toward the body's midline.	Hip (when a leg is brought back toward the midline)
Extension	To increase the angle at a joint. This straightens a limb toward its maximum length.	Elbow (when movement at the elbow brings the forearm down and extends the arm) Knee (when movement at the knee straightens the leg to its full length)
Flexion	To decrease the angle at a joint.	Elbow (when movement at the elbow bends the arm so that the forearm is closer to the bicep) Knee (when movement at the knee bends the leg) Fingers (when fingers are closed together in a fist)

The act of pitching a ball involves a combination of joint movements.

Special joint movements include plantar flexion, which is a movement of the foot away from the lower leg. Good examples are pointing the toes in ballet (dancing *en pointe*) or pressing on the gas pedal of a car. Bringing the foot back toward the leg is called dorsiflexion. Other special joint movements of the feet are inversion, which is moving the sole of the foot toward the body's midline, and eversion, which is moving the sole away from the midline.

Special movements at the wrist include pronation, referring to a movement in which the palm of the hand turns down to the posterior position, as though you are flapping your hand wrist down. Supination, occurs when the palm is turned forward or upward, as though you are motioning for someone to stop.

Another special joint movement is called circumduction. One example is the pitching motion of a baseball player when his arm is rotated in full circles about the shoulder. This motion is one in which flexion, abduction, extension, and adduction movements are combined in sequence.

MINERAL AND CHEMICAL WAREHOUSING

Bones are the warehouses that store most of the body's calcium, phosphorous, and other essential minerals. If there is not enough calcium in the diet for the body to maintain appropriate levels of minerals and chemicals in its fluids, the body will go to its storehouse in the bones.

Calcium is the most abundant mineral in the human body, which contains roughly 2.2 to 4.4 pounds (1 to 2 kg) of calcium, 98 percent of which is found in the bones in the form of calcium phosphate crystals. The remaining 2 percent is distributed throughout the body and is essential to functions such as the contraction of muscles and sending signals through the nerves. The skeletal system acts as a reservoir that maintains the equilibrium of calcium and phosphorous in the bloodstream. Without this balancing act, serious health issues can occur.

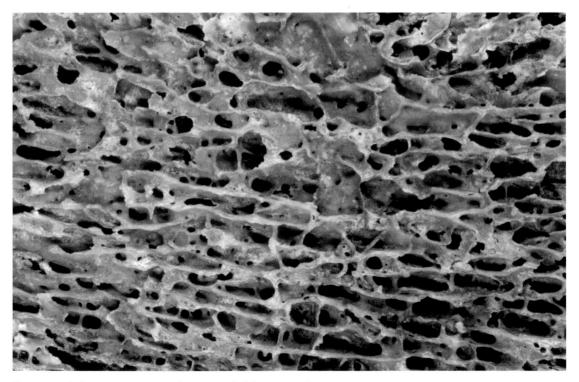

Bone matrix houses many nutrients needed for strong bones.

Even small changes in normal concentrations will have some effect on cellular operations. Larger changes can cause a serious medical problem. Too many calcium ions in the bloodstream, called hypercalcemia, may cause a heart attack. Too few calcium ions in the bloodstream—called hypocalcemia—may cause respiratory problems. A 50 percent reduction in calcium concentrations generally leads to death. However, such significant disturbances in calcium metabolism are fairly rare because calcium ion concentrations usually are closely regulated by the body.

Besides calcium and phosphorous, other minerals stored in bones include potassium, manganese, magnesium, silica, iron, zinc, selenium, and boron, to name just a few. In order for bones to absorb the minerals, vitamin D must be present in a person's diet.

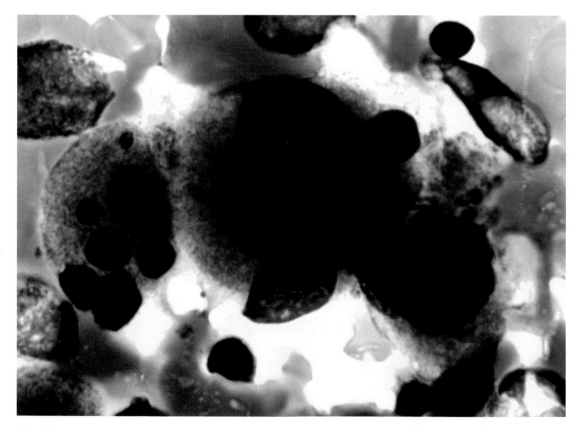

Blood production can be affected if bone cells are damaged or malnourished. Bone marrow cells are also responsible for producing platelets (dark purple) that help the blood clot.

BLOOD CELL AND PLATELET PRODUCTION

A vital function of the skeletal system is the production of red and white blood cells. The hollow spaces in living bone are home to connective tissue called marrow. Red marrow consists of a mixture of blood cells and platelets and the stem cells that produce them. Platelets are important for assisting in blood clotting by sticking to other platelets and to damaged tissue. Stem cells form blood cells in a process called hematopoiesis. Important sites of blood cell formation include the cancellous, or spongy, material at the proximal ends of the femur and humerus; the sternum; ribs; vertebrae; pelvis; skull; and scapula. About 175 billion red cells are produced each day and are released as needed by the body. These red blood cells, or RBCs as they are sometimes called, help to carry oxygen around the body.

Yellow marrow contains large numbers of fat cells and is found in the cavity in the shafts of long bones. These bones store energy reserves as lipids in areas of yellow marrow. If a body suffers from anemia—a shortage of oxygen-carrying red blood cells—yellow marrow can be converted to red marrow for the production of the needed red blood cells.

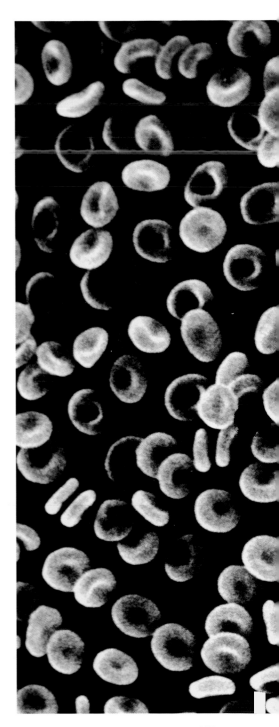

Healthy red blood cells are shaped like rounded disks.

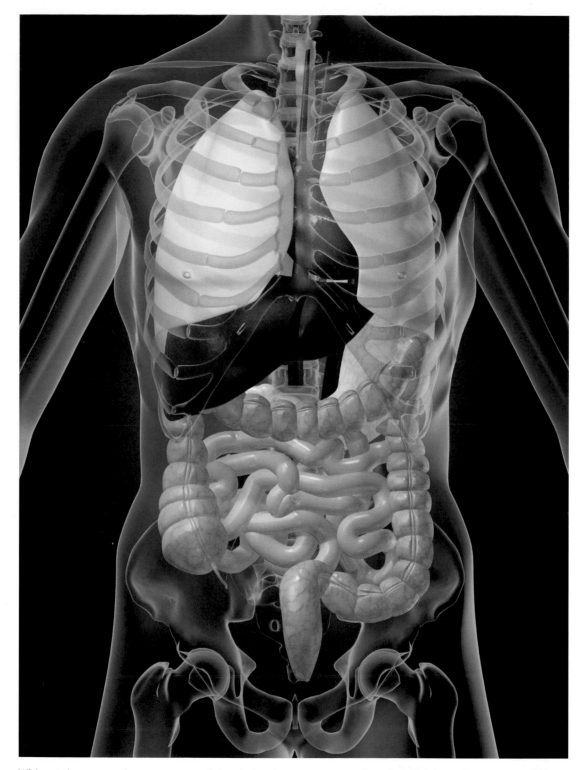

Without the supportive structures of the skeletal system, most of our fragile internal organs would be easily damaged.

CLUES TO THE PAST

The skeletal system is also useful long after it has been alive. Many types of scientists gain valuable information from bones. Fossilized bones unearthed by archaeologists in Africa have shown that the human skull has evolved drastically over two million years. Skeletal remains also show that early humans had a short thumb, which undoubtedly made grasping and manipulating objects awkward and clumsy.

The science of human paleopathology is the study of disease in ancient populations. The study is performed by examining fossilized human skeletal remains. In addition to providing evidence of disease, bones that have arrowheads or fragments of other weapons embedded in them show evidence of warfare in the culture. A lot of information about not only an individual, but an entire society can be learned from the study of bones.

In modern times, the art of facial reconstruction is a method used in forensic anthropology to aid in the identification of skeletal remains. While this method is often used as a last resort to identify the skeletal remains of an unidentified person, it is a good illustration of the importance of the skeletal system in all phases of life and death.

These skeletons were found in a gravesite that is more than 2,000 years old.

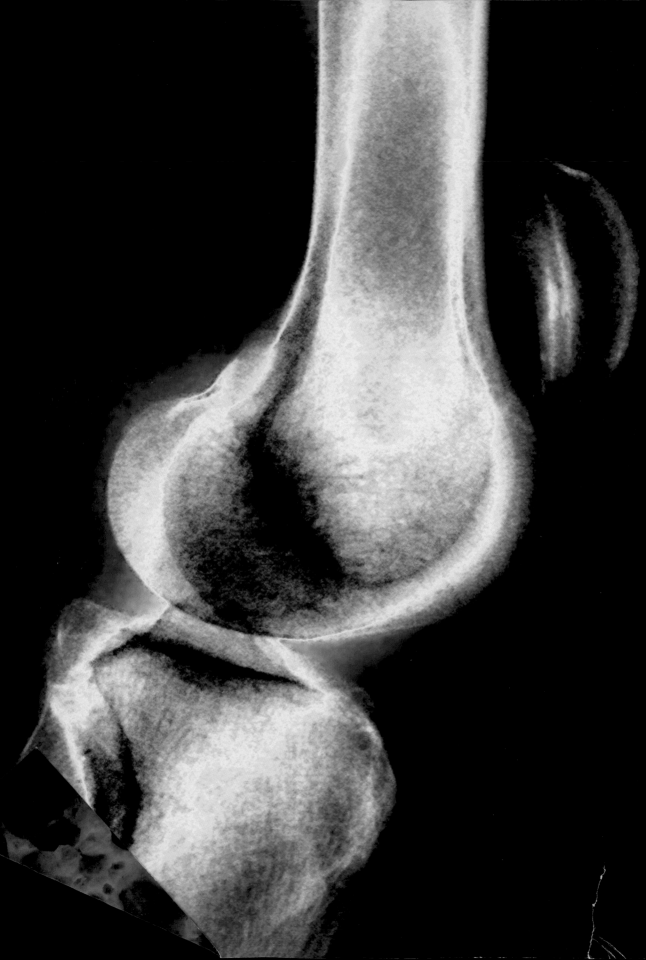

4

When the Skeletal System Fails

The skeletal system is built to withstand the pressures and stresses of daily living, protecting the body's delicate inner organs in the process. Sometimes, however, the system can be stressed beyond its capacity and injuries can result.

BROKEN BONES

No matter how strong a bone is, if enough force is exerted on it, a bone can be broken. This can happen if a person falls, twists or bends the bone or joint incorrectly, or if the bone has been weakened from injury, disease, or poor health. Any bone in the body can be broken.

This X ray shows a dislocated knee cap. As a result of an injury, the knee cap (small bone to the right) has been forced into an abnormal position.

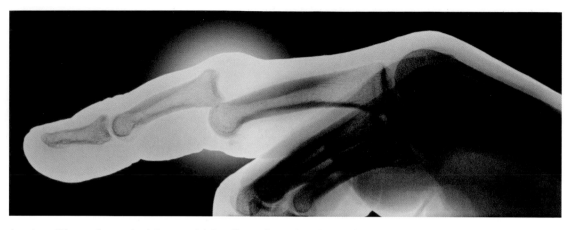

A colored X ray shows the joint at which a finger bone has been dislocated.

The collarbone, or clavicle, is the most frequently broken bone. This is because it often receives the full force of falls on outstretched arms or blows to the shoulder.

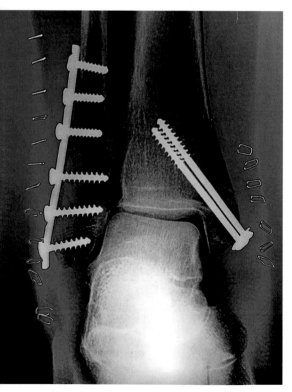

Sometimes treatment for a broken bone requires inserting metal plates or screws to hold the bones in their proper places.

When a joint is pushed out of place it is often said that it is dislocated. Dislocated joints are common injuries for people of many ages. Jamming a finger against a volleyball or basketball can cause one of the finger joints to be dislocated. Shoulder joints are also commonly dislocated. Treatment usually involves forcing the bones back into place. A brace or splint is often used to make sure the joint stays in place during healing.

Treatment

There are different forms of treatment for broken bones. It depends upon the age of the patient, the type of bone or joint involved, and the extent of damage. Broken bones can be very painful so doctors will almost

Common Fractures

Bones can break—or fracture—in different ways. When dealing with a broken bone, medical professionals try to identify the type of fracture so that the right form of treatment can be used. Here are some common examples of different types of fractures.

Comminuted	Bone has been shattered into many fragments. This fracture could result from an automobile crash or a gunshot wound.
Compound	Bone has been broken and an end of the bone protrudes through the skin and is visible. Sometimes called an open fracture.
Compression	Bone has been crushed. This often occurs in vertebrae subjected to severe stresses, such as when a person lands on his or her backside in a fall.
Greenstick	Bone has not been broken completely, but only one side of the shaft is broken and the other is bent, similar to the way a green stick or twig breaks. Generally occurs in children whose long bones have not yet ossified completely.
Impacted	Bone has been broken and a fragment of the bone has been firmly driven into the cancellous tissue of another fragment.
Simple	Bone has been broken cleanly and does not penetrate or break the skin and neighboring tissues are not damaged. Also called a closed fracture.
Spiral	Produced by twisting pressures, bone has been twisted apart along the length of the bone.
Stress	Tiny breaks, or hairline cracks, in the bone, usually caused by repetitive stress from activities like running, pitching, or rowing. Common overuse injury.

always give some sort of pain medication to give the patient some relief. Stress fractures are usually left alone to heal. In most cases of broken bones, the bones will need to be re-set and put back into their proper place. Depending upon the injury, special braces or casts worn on different parts of the body can accomplish this. In more serious cases, re-setting the bone requires surgery to insert pins, rods, or other forms of support for the bone.

If you think you have broken a bone you must see a doctor as soon as possible. Not only can the doctor help you with the pain, but your chance of recovery is better if you are under medical supervision. Broken bones that are not treated can cause infections, can injure nerves or organs, and can heal improperly. An improperly healed bone can cause your body to become deformed, can limit your mobility, or can cause bone problems later in life.

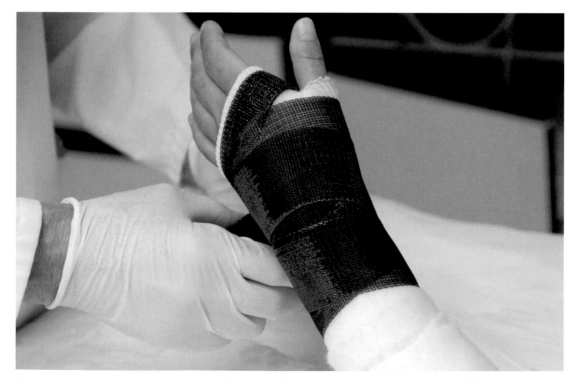

A doctor puts a cast on a broken wrist. The cast will help to keep the bones in place while they heal.

Sports Injuries

Many broken bones are the results of sport injuries. Direct hits by opposing players, painful falls while reaching for a ball, and overextending the body to score a point or defend a goal are just some of the ways athletes can injure their bones. Studies have shown that sports injuries are on the rise in children and teenagers in the United States. Each year more than 3.5 million children under the age of fifteen require medical treatment due to sport-related injuries.

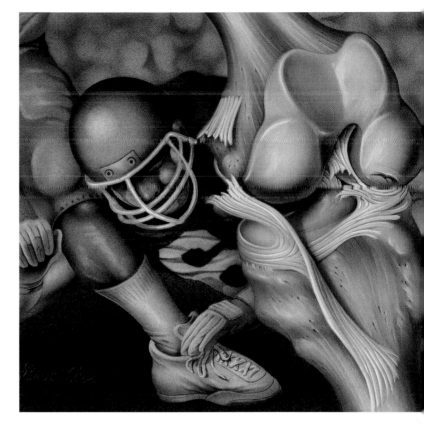

This illustration shows how a hit to the knee can injure the ligaments, tendons, and muscles that hold knee bones in place.

More children and adolescents than ever are participating in the same sport year-round, and as a result many young athletes are developing overuse injuries. Overuse, or chronic, injuries—about half of the sports injuries that happen to middle school and high school students—usually occur over a period of time with repetitive motion or impact. The injuries vary from chronic muscle strains and tendonitis to stress fractures. Stress fractures are weak spots or small cracks in the bone. For example, stress fractures in the foot may come from training for soccer, basketball, track, football, and other sports. The bones in the metatarsals in runners, ballet dancers, and basketball players are especially vulnerable to stress fractures.

How Can a Sports Injury Be Prevented?

Sports injuries are often the result of inadequate training or structural defects or weaknesses in the body. Around 60 percent of those who begin a new sport or exercise sustain a sports injury within the first six weeks. With the proper training and precautions, however, sports injuries can often be prevented. Here is a list of basic steps you should follow to prevent a sports injury:

- Stretch and warm up properly before any physical activity.

- Drink plenty of fluids and rest when possible during a game or during a workout.

- Exercise different muscle groups and exercise every other day to reduce injuries caused by overuse.

- Stretch and cool down properly after exercising or playing sports.

- On a regular basis, perform stretching exercises to improve the muscles' ability to contract and perform, reducing the risk for injury.

- The appropriate shoes and shoe supports may correct certain foot problems that can lead to injury.

- Wear the necessary protective gear, such as helmets, shin guards, and mouth guards

- If you suffer an injury and the pain increases with activity (sports medicine doctors call this an "upward crescendo") and causes swelling, limping, or loss of range of motion, see a doctor as soon as possible.

- If you have been injured or are recovering from an injury, make sure you are well enough before resuming strenuous activity.

ARTHRITIS

There are several diseases and disorders of the bones and joints, in addition to fractures and breaks, that can sideline a person from doing favorite activities. One of the oldest known conditions is arthritis, or swollen and inflamed joints. For thousands of years, people have been suffering from the pain, swelling, and stiffness caused by arthritis. Studies of archaeological finds in what is now Tennessee show that arthritis in the 6,500-year-old remains of ancient American Indians is the same as the rheumatoid arthritis suffered by people today. Excavations of pyramids and tombs that are more than four thousand years old unearthed evidence of arthritis in the remains of mummified Egyptians.

Osteoarthritis

Arthritis is a generic term for more than one hundred medical conditions that affect nearly 46 million adults and 300,000 children in the United States alone. It is a disease of the joints, and the symptoms include stiffness, inflammation, and damage to joint cartilage and surrounding bone. Cartilage and bone are damaged as the bones rub together and deformity results when one side of the joint collapses more than the other side. When the cartilage loss is great, there may be severe pain in the involved joint. One example of arthritis is juvenile arthritis, which causes joint inflammation and stiffness in children sixteen years old and younger.

The most common form is osteoarthritis, which usually affects people over the age of sixty. The knee is the most commonly affected joint, followed by the hip, shoulder, hands, and elbow. It is now thought that osteoarthritis is caused by wear and tear, overuse, injury, and obesity. Genetics and heredity can also determine whether or not a person develops osteoarthritis. Certain foods may also trigger a chemical reaction in the body similar to an allergic response. Chemicals are released causing

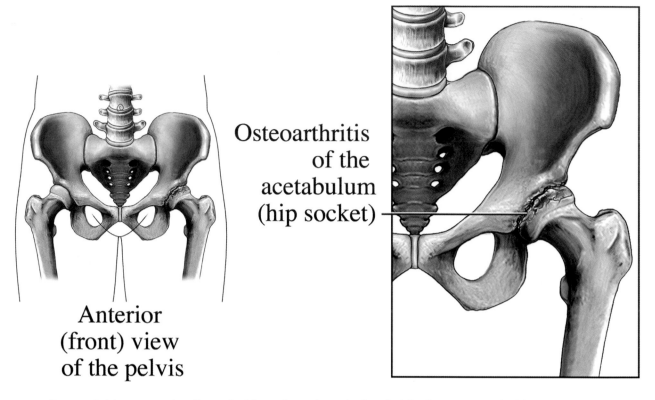

Osteoarthritis
of the
acetabulum
(hip socket)

Anterior
(front) view
of the pelvis

Osteoarthritis commonly affects the hip socket, where the head of the femur meets the hip bone.

inflammation in the joints and, eventually, arthritis. Often, when these trigger foods are removed from the diet, arthritis subsides. Medical research has shown that a diet high in animal and dairy fat and refined foods (white flour, sugar, and salt, for example) prevent the body from absorbing badly needed nutrients. This absorption failure causes a body reaction that leads to arthritis.

There are at least three important steps you can take to prevent osteoarthritis: weight control, injury prevention, and exercise. A diet that focuses on fruits, vegetables, and whole grains will not only help the body absorb needed nutrients that prevent inflammation, but will also help to control a healthy weight. Losing extra pounds usually leads to some relief from arthritis pain. Researchers have found that overweight women can "significantly lower their risk for developing osteoarthritis of the knee by losing weight."

Protecting joints from serious injury or repeated minor injuries is key to decreasing the risk of damaging cartilage in the joints. "Repeated minor injuries" include job-related activities like frequent kneeling, squatting, or other postures that place stress on the knee joint.

Light to moderate exercise not only reduces the risk of developing osteoarthritis, but will also help to relieve the pain and inflammation of those who suffer from it. Careful weight lifting, walking, tai chi, yoga, biking, swimming, and aqua aerobics can all be helpful. Research shows that even modest weight loss combined with exercise is more effective in decreasing the pain of arthritis and restoring joint function than either weight loss or exercise alone. Also, acupuncture—a treatment in which fine needles are inserted into specific parts of the body—is increasingly being used to reduce osteoarthritis pain.

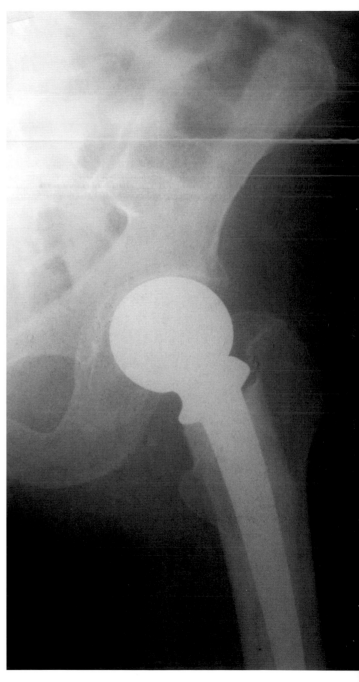

Sometimes when bones are damaged beyond repair, artificial parts can be used to replace the bone. The head of this person's femur was replaced with a special metal piece that fits into the hip socket.

Rheumatoid Arthritis

Rheumatoid arthritis is another type of arthritis, and it typically affects the same joints on both sides of the body, such as the hands, wrists, feet, knees, ankles, shoulders, neck, jaw, and elbows. Rheumatoid arthritis is one of the most common autoimmune disorders, which are diseases caused when the immune system attacks the body's own tissues. Autoimmune reactions may be set off by infection, tissue injury, or emotional trauma in those with a genetic tendency to suffer from them. Still's disease, which is also known as systemic juvenile rheumatoid arthritis, affects between 10 and 20 percent of all children with juvenile rheumatoid arthritis. In addition to the joint pain typical of rheumatoid arthritis, symptoms of Still's disease include high-spiking daily fevers (104 degrees Fahrenheit or higher) and fatigue.

There is no known way to prevent rheumatoid arthritis because the exact cause of the disease is not known. However, there are strategies that can help control the painful symptoms of rheumatoid arthritis. Many doctors recommend following a low-protein, high-carbohydrate

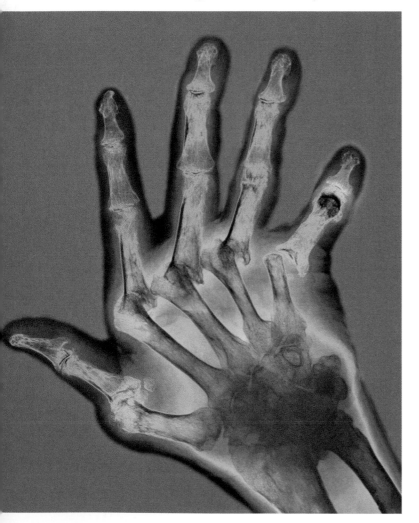

Severe rheumatoid arthritis has seriously deformed this woman's hand.

diet; minimizing how much meat is eaten; eliminating milk and milk products; and increasing intake of omega-3 fatty acids by eating more cold water fish and walnuts. Treatment for systemic juvenile rheumatoid arthritis is usually directed at the specific areas of inflammation. These treatments may involve medication that reduces swelling, such as prednisone. Aspirin and other non-steroidal anti-inflammatory medications (NSAIDs) can also help. In addition, an anti-inflammatory diet and taking a fish oil supplement is recommended.

SLIPPED CAPITAL FEMORAL EPIPHYSIS

Slipped capital femoral epiphysis (SCFE) is an unusual, but not uncommon, disorder of the hip. For reasons that are not well understood, the ball at the upper end of the femur slips off in a backward direction due to weakness of the growth plate. Most often, it develops during periods of accelerated growth, shortly after the onset of puberty, usually between the ages of eleven and sixteen.

SCFE occurs two to three times more often in boys than in girls, and a large number of patients are overweight for their height. The slipping of the epiphysis may be a slow and gradual process, or it may occur suddenly and be associated with a minor fall or trauma.

Once diagnosed, treatment should be immediate in order to stabilize the hip. Surgery is the treatment of choice with this disorder. The orthopedic surgeon will insert a screw into the femur to hold the bone in place. Children who suffered from SCFE when they are young may develop arthritis in the hip when they grow older.

OSTEOMYELITIS

Osteomyelitis is a painful, severe infection in a bone, usually caused by bacteria from one of the following situations: an open injury to the bone,

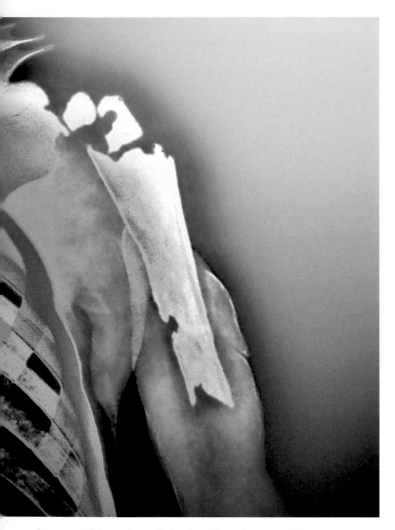

Osteomyelitis—a bone infection—has destroyed the upper section of this child's humerus.

such as a compound fracture; an infection from elsewhere in the body that has spread to the bone through the blood; a minor trauma that may lead to a blood clot around the bone, followed by an infection due to bacteria; bacteria in the bloodstream that results in the destruction of the bone; or a chronic open wound or soft tissue infection that eventually extends down to the bone surface, leading to a bone infection.

Osteomyelitis affects about two out of every 10,000 people. If left untreated, the infection can become chronic and cause a loss of blood supply to the affected bone. When this happens, it can lead to the eventual death of the bone tissue. In children, the long bones are usually affected.

In adults, the vertebrae and the pelvis are most commonly affected. Risk factors include recent trauma, diabetes, treatments for diabetes that require removing wastes from blood (called hemodialysis), and intravenous drug abuse. People who have had their spleen—an organ that filters, stores, and destroys blood cells—removed are also at higher risk for osteomyelitis.

RICKETS

Rickets affects children who are vitamin D_3 deficient. Usually, these children are rarely exposed to sunlight and do not consume enough vitamin D in the foods they eat. Vitamin D helps the body properly control calcium and phosphate levels. If the blood levels of calcium and phosphate become too low, the body will produce hormones that take away these minerals from the bones. This then leads to weak and soft bones. The bones of children with rickets are so poorly mineralized that they become flexible. Their femurs, tibias, and fibulas bend under the weight of their bodies. As a result, many children with rickets develop a bow-legged appearance.

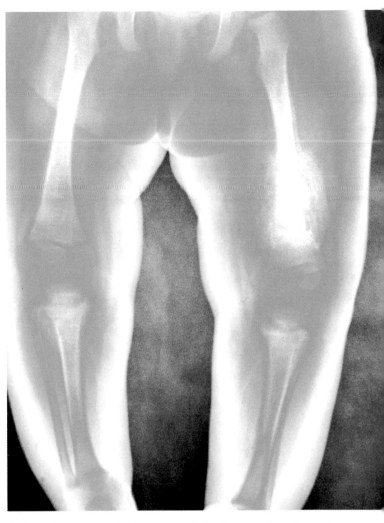

Rickets have caused this young child to become bow-legged.

Besides healthy exposure to sunlight, good sources of vitamin D_3 include milk, eggs, salmon, tuna, mackerel, sardines, and cod liver oil.

SCOLIOSIS

During childhood and adolescence, the spine can become abnormally distorted. To aid in flexibility and balance, the spine should curve gently front to back, but it should not curve sideways. Scoliosis is one of the most

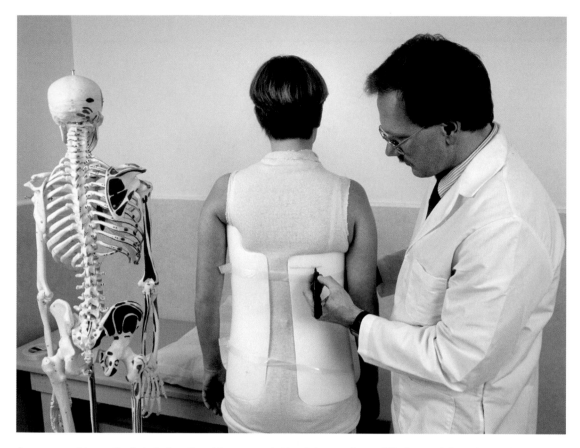

A woman with scoliosis is being fitted for a special back brace that will help straighten her spine.

well known spinal-curvature disorders. A spine affected by scoliosis has an abnormal lateral, or sideways, curvature. The most common type of scoliosis, called idiopathic scoliosis, has no known cause, and there is no known prevention. Once a patient has been diagnosed with scoliosis, there are several issues to consider when discussing treatment. Depending upon how the spine is curved—and where the curve is—there are three basic types of scoliosis treatment: nonsurgical observation (in moderate cases, watching and seeing what happens); orthopedic bracing (to slowly correct the curve and support the body); or surgery (usually reserved for serious cases or cases that can easily be corrected through surgery).

SPINA BIFIDA

From the Latin, meaning "split spine" or "open spine," spina bifida is a disabling birth defect of the vertebrae. During the first month of development of the embryo, before birth, the vertebral laminae fail to unite. Laminae are the thinnest, flattest parts of the arches of each vertebra. As a result, damage to the spinal cord and and nerves around the spine can occur. Spina bifida affects nearly one out of every 1,000 newborns in the United States.

There are different types of spina bifida. In mild cases, the condition may pass unnoticed. In other forms, there may be no nerve damage, and individuals may suffer minor disabilities and some nerve problems later in life. In extreme cases most of the spinal column is affected, which causes nerve damage and severe disabilities. Sometimes people who suffer from spina bifida can become paralyzed from the nerve and spinal cord damage.

A B vitamin called folic acid can help prevent spina bifida because it helps to build healthy cells. Studies show that if all women in the United States took the recommended amount of folic acid every day before and during early pregnancy, a high percentage of diseases—like spina bifida—could be prevented.

AGING AND THE SKELETAL SYSTEM

The bones of the skeleton become thinner and weaker as a normal part of the aging process. Inadequate ossification is called osteopenia and we all become somewhat osteopenic as we grow older. This reduction in bone mass begins between the ages of thirty and forty when there is a loss of calcium salts and a decrease in the amount of protein formed in bone tissue. Muscle tissue is also lost throughout adult life, which results in the tendency to eliminate physical exercise from daily activities. This reduction in physical activity further weakens bones and joints.

Osteoporosis

Osteoporosis, the most common bone disease, is a condition characterized by a loss of bone mass that causes bones to become porous and fragile. The degree of mineralization of the bone matrix—bone density—usually increases until about the age of thirty. When more bone material is lost than can be rebuilt, bones become brittle and easily fractured. In 2004, a U.S. surgeon general's report warned that by 2020, half of all Americans older than fifty will be at risk for fractures from osteoporosis and low bone mass if no immediate action is taken. The report stated that 10 million Americans over the age of fifty have osteoporosis, while another 34 million are at risk for developing it. Each year, nearly 1.5 million people

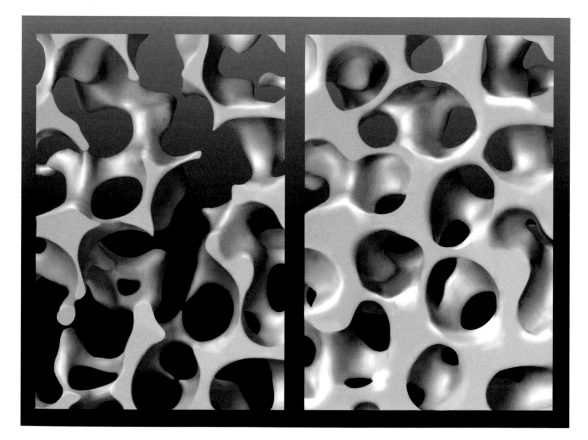

A computer illustration shows osteoporotic bone (left) and normal healthy bone (right).

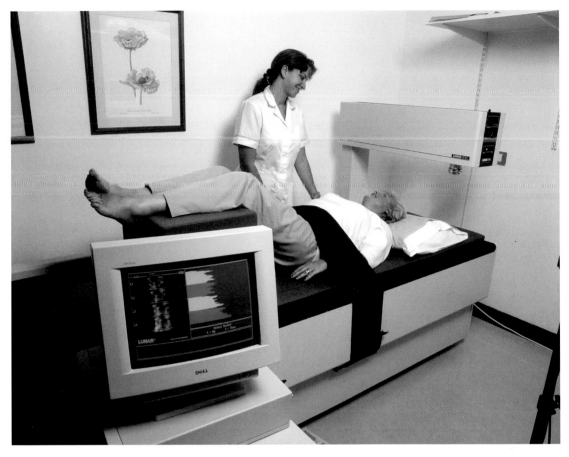

Bone density scans can help a doctor determine if a person has osteoporosis.

suffer a bone fracture related to osteoporosis. These broken bones occur typically in the hip, spine, and wrist. Around 80 percent of Americans with osteoporosis are women.

Although the symptoms show up later in life, young women may be living a lifestyle that inevitably leads to porous and brittle bones. Constant dieting—which results in a lack of proper nutrition that includes adequate calcium and vitamin D intake—and over- or under-exercising set the stage for this disease. Other risk factors include smoking; being too thin; drinking excessive amounts of alcohol or caffeine; being inactive or bedridden; suffering from an eating disorder such as anorexia nervosa or bulimia nervosa; a family history of osteoporosis; long-term use of corticosteroids, such as prednisone or hydrocortisone for inflammatory conditions, or acid-suppressing medications for heartburn; being Caucasian or Asian; and prolonged amenorrhea (lack of menstrual period) from rigorous athletic training.

Medication can be given to help with osteoporosis, and surgery can be performed to fix some bones broken from osteoporosis. But experts agree that the best way to fight osteoporosis is by being healthy and taking care of your bones and body.

BONE TUMORS AND CANCER

Tumors are the result of abnormal cell growth. They may be benign (noncancerous) or malignant (cancerous). Benign tumors do not spread and are rarely life-threatening. However, benign tumors may grow and interfere with healthy bone tissue. Malignant tumors usually spread to other parts of the body and are very likely to cause serious health problems.

Cancer that starts in a bone—called primary bone cancer—is rare, with approximately 2,500 new cases diagnosed each year in the United States. Cancer that has spread to the bone from another part of the body—secondary bone cancer—is more common. It is not certain what causes bone cancer, but a number of things may put a person at risk. These include radiation or chemotherapy treatments for other conditions, having hereditary bone problems, or suffering from Paget's disease. With Paget's disease, old bone breaks down faster than new bone can be built to replace it. Over time, the body overcompensates by building new bone at a faster than normal rate. This rapid remodeling produces softer- and weaker-than-normal bone, which can lead to bone pain, deformities, and fractures.

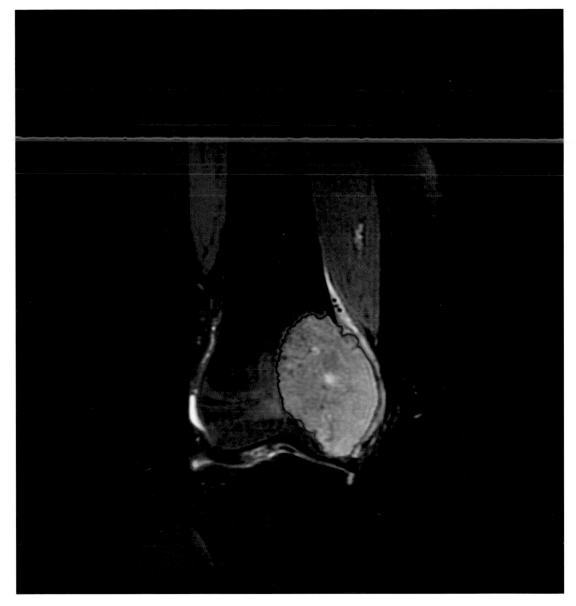

A scan shows a bone tumor (blue) located at the end of the femur, near the knee joint.

The most common symptom of bone cancer is pain, but other symptoms include fatigue, fever, weight loss, and anemia. It is important to note that none of these symptoms is a definite sign of cancer. Several different types of tests, X rays, and scans need to be done before a doctor can determine

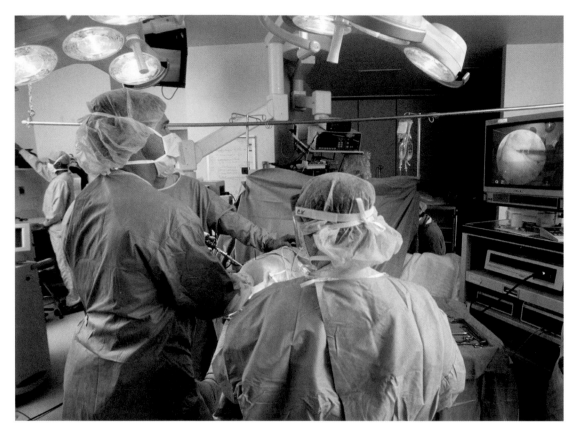

Surgery can be used to treat many different types of bone conditions. Arthroscopic surgery, which uses a small tube and camera to look at joints and bones, allows doctors to fix bones without opening up a large portion of a patient's body.

if a person has bone cancer. If cancer of the bone is diagnosed, surgery to remove tumors is often the main treatment. Other treatments include amputation (surgically removing body parts that are deteriorating from the cancer), chemotherapy (treatment with cancer-fighting drugs), and radiation therapy (treatment with special X rays).

Cancers of the Bone

TYPES OF CANCER	TISSUE OF ORIGIN	COMMON LOCATIONS	COMMON AGES
Osteosarcoma	Osteoid	Knees, upper legs, upper arms; develops in growing bones	10-25 years old
Chondrosarcoma	Cartilage	Pelvis, upper legs, shoulders; starts in cartilage	50-60 years old
Ewing's Sarcoma	Immature nerve tissue, usually in bone marrow	Pelvis, upper legs, ribs, arms; begins in nerve tissue in bone marrow of young people, often after treatment of another condition with radiation or chemotherapy	10-20 years old

Adapted from http:// www.cancer.gov

5

Maintaining a Healthy Skeletal System

The strength and health of our bones depends on good nutrition and regular exercise. These things should begin in early childhood and continue throughout life.

WHAT NOT TO DO

Do not smoke! Several studies have identified smoking as a risk factor for osteoporosis and bone fracture. Smokers who fracture their bones usually take longer to heal than nonsmokers. Additionally, smokers may experience more complications during the healing process.

Taking calcium—by drinking milk or eating dairy products— is one of the many ways you can strengthen your bones.

Smoking can also hurt nonsmokers who spend time with smokers. At least one study suggests that exposure to second-hand smoke during youth and early adulthood may increase the risk of developing low bone mass.

Avoid consuming too many caffeinated products, such as coffee, soda, milk chocolate candy bars, and over-the-counter weight-control drugs. They can increase the loss of calcium through the kidneys and drain off skeletal calcium.

Avoid carbonated soft drinks, or soda. High consumption of carbonated soft drinks during adolescence may reduce bone mineral growth and therefore increase fracture risk. These drinks are also usually high in sugar and can cause weight gain, which can further stress a person's bones.

WATCH YOUR CALCIUM

Calcium phosphate in the bone matrix is required for bone to be physically strong. The higher the calcium phosphate content, the stronger and healthier the bone is. For calcium phosphate to be added to the matrix, it must first be absorbed into the bloodstream from your diet. Calcium is an essential dietary element, and is necessary for the maintenance of the normal heartbeat, blood clotting, and for the normal functioning of nerves and muscles. Typically, blood calcium is used for these processes before it is stored in the bones. If calcium and phosphorous are in short supply from dietary intake, the bones generally do not receive enough calcium for storage. In fact, if not enough dietary calcium is available, the body pulls stored calcium out of the bones to ensure muscle, nerve, and blood clotting function. Overall, the amount of calcium in the bloodstream and the amount available to the bones for storage depends upon complex hormonal mechanisms, as well as the presence of adequate blood levels of vitamins A and D.

Most people do not realize that you can also get some calcium through broccoli. Eating this green vegetable has other health benefits as well.

The development of strong, healthy bones throughout the skeletal system must begin in childhood. For most people, bone mass peaks by their late twenties. By that time, bones have reached their maximum strength and density. Up to 90 percent of peak bone mass is acquired by age eighteen in girls and age twenty in boys, which makes youth the best time to invest in bone health.

An abundant source of calcium in the American diet is dairy products like milk and cheese. It is not essential that a person's source of calcium be only dairy products, as there are many other sources of calcium. Non-dairy foods rich in calcium include figs; almonds; sesame seeds and sesame tahini; baked beans; soy nuts; broccoli; greens, such as collards, mustard, kale, turnip greens, and bok choy; canned salmon (with bones) and sardines; calcium-fortified soy milk; and blackstrap molasses. If you do not get enough calcium from food sources, a calcium supplement might help. Always talk to your doctor or nutritionist before deciding to take any kind of supplements. He or she can determine what kind of supplement— and how much—you should take. Taking too many supplements can actually hurt your body.

MOVE THAT BODY!

The maintenance of a healthy skeleton is a lifelong effort. The process of building sound bone tissue requires consistent, regular exercise. Healthy physical stress on the bones that occurs during vigorous exercise—especially during periods of growth—increases calcium deposits at points where the bone is under stress. In short, exercising makes your bones grow stronger.

All bones respond to exercise by increasing in size and strength. Two types of exercises are important for building and maintaining bone mass: weight-bearing and resistance exercises. Weight-bearing exercises cause bones and muscles to work against gravity, when the feet and legs bear

Exercise gets your heart pumping while also strengthening your bones and muscles.

the weight. Weight-bearing exercises include running, walking, playing basketball or soccer, and dancing. Swimming and cycling are not weight bearing, but they are good for your body in many other ways.

Resistance exercises use muscular strength to improve muscle mass and to strengthen bone. These activities include weight lifting—such as using the free weights and weight machines found in gyms—and exercises using your own weight for resistance, like push-ups, crunches, lunges, and squats.

Building healthy bones begins at birth and should last your whole life. But it is never too late to start taking care of your body. Exercise regularly. Eat healthy foods. The old saying definitely applies to your skeletal system: Use it or lose it!

Stronger muscles usually mean stronger bones. Strengthening your bones now can help you maintain a healthy skeletal system for the rest of your life.

Glossary

appendicular skeleton—The components of the vertebrate skeleton that are attached to the main supporting, or axial, skeleton. The appendicular skeleton is made up of paired appendages (for example, legs and arms) together with the pelvic and pectoral girdles.

arthritis—Inflammation of one or more joints.

articulating—Meeting at a joint or articulation.

axial skeleton—The skeleton of the trunk and head.

bone marrow—Connective tissue that occupies the cavities and cancellous part of most bones.

cartilage—A fibrous and elastic connective tissue that covers the ends of bones in a joint.

collagen—The protein substance found in skin, tendon, bone, cartilage and all other connective tissue.

diaphysis—The main or midsection of a long bone.

epiphysis—The end of a long bone that is originally separated from the main bone by a layer of cartilage but later becomes united to the main bone through ossification.

femur—The bone of the leg situated between the pelvis and knee. It is the largest and strongest bone in the body.

fibrous joint—An immovable joint (especially between the bones of the skull).

fontanels—Soft membranous gap between the immature skull bones of an infant or fetus.

Haversian canal—Any of the tiny, interconnecting, longitudinal channels in bone tissue through which blood vessels, nerve fibers, and lymphatics pass.

hematopoiesis—The formation of blood or blood cells in the body.

lacuna—A small cavity within the bone matrix, containing an osteocyte.

lamina—A bone that forms the arched part of a vertebra. Laminae is the plural form of lamina.

ligament—A band of connective tissue that connects a bone to another bone.

matrix—The intercellular substance of bone, consisting of collagenous fibers, ground substance, and inorganic salts.

medullary cavity—The space within a bone that contains the marrow.

osseous tissue—A strong connective tissue containing specialized cells and a mineralized matrix of calcium phosphate and calcium carbonate.

ossification or **ossified**—The formation of bone; formed bone.

osteoblasts—A cell that produces the fibers and matrix of bone.

osteoclast—A cell that dissolves the fibers and matrix of bone.

osteocytes—A bone cell responsible for the maintenance and turnover of the mineral content of the surrounding bone.

osteoid—The organic matrix of bone; young bone that has not undergone calcification.

osteopenia—Any decrease in bone mass below the normal.

osteoporosis—A disease characterized by decrease in bone mass and density.

pectoral—Relating to or situated in the breast or chest.

periosteum—A specialized connective tissue covering all bones and having bone-forming potentialities.

resorption—The process by which bone tissue is broken down and removed by osteoclasts.

trabeculae—Needle-like threads of spongy bone that surround a network of spaces.

yellow marrow—A type of marrow—found in the ends of long bones in adults—that stores fats used for energy. Yellow marrow can also be converted to red marrow for blood cell production.

Find Out More

Books

Ballard, Carol. *Bones*. Chicago: Heinemann Library, 2003.

Hoffmann, Gretchen. *Osteoporosis*. New York: Marshall Cavendish Benchmark, 2008.

Sayler, Mary Harwell. *The Encyclopedia of the Muscle and Skeletal Systems and Disorders*. New York: Facts on File, 2005.

Simon, Seymour. *Bones: Our Skeletal System*. New York: HarperCollins Publishers, 2000.

Walker, Pam and Elaine Wood. *The Skeletal and Muscular System*. San Diego, CA: Lucent Books, 2003.

Web Sites

Bones, Muscles, and Joints: The Musculoskeletal System
http://www.kidshealth.org/teen/your_body/body_basics/bones_muscles_joints.html

National Bone Health Campaign
http://www.cdc.gov/powerfulbones

Nutrition for Everyone: Bone Health
http://cdc.gov/nccdphp/dnpa/nutrition/nutrition_for_everyone/bonehealth

Osteoporosis Tutorial
http://nlm.nih.gov/medlineplus/tutorials/osteoporosis/htm/_no_50_no_0.htm

The Skeletal System
http://yucky.discovery.com/noflash/body/pg000124.html

Teens' Health: Dealing with Sports Injuries
http://www.kidshealth.org/teen/food_fitness/sports/sports_injuries.html

Bibliography

The American Society for Bone and Mineral Research.
  http://www.asbmr.org

Blakemore, Colin and and Sheila Jennett. *The Oxford Companion to the
  Body*. NewYork: Oxford University Press, 2001.

Bronowski, J. *The Ascent of Man*. Boston: Little, Brown and Company,
  1973.

Center for Disease Control. "Folic Acid and Prevention of Spina Bifida and
  Anencephaly." http"//www.cdc.gov/mmwr/PDF/rr/rr5113.pdf

"Early Clinical Pathologists." 4: John Hunter (1728-1793). S Lakhani,
  J Clin Pathol. 1991 August; 44(8): 621-623.

Faller, Adolf and Michael Schuenke. *The Human Body: An Introduction to
  Structure and Function*. New York: Thieme Medical Publishers, 2004.

Kent, Michael. *The Oxford Dictionary of Sport Science and Medicine*. new
  York: Oxford University Press, 2007.

Martini, Frederic H. *Fundamentals of Anatomy and Physiology*. Upper
  Saddle River, NJ: Prentice Hall, 1998.

Miller, Jonathan. *The Body in Question*. New York: Random House, 1978.

Shapiro, Leonard. "The Hit That Changed a Career: 20 Years Later,
  Theismann Reflects on Incident." *Washington Post,* November 18, 2005

Spina Bifida Association. http://www.sbaa.org

Steele, D. Gentry and Claud A. Bramblett. *The Anatomy and Biology of the
  Human Skeleton*. College Station, TX: Texas A&M University Press, 1988.

U.S. Department of Agriculture. *Food and Nutrition Information Center*.
  http://www.nal.usda.gov/fnic

U.S. Department of Health & Human Services. "Bone Health and
  Osteoporosis: A Report of the Surgeon General (2004)."
  http://www.surgeongeneral.gov/library/bonehealth/content.html

U.S. National Institutes of Health (NIH) *PubMed Central*.
  http://www.pubmedcentral.nih.gov

Weil, Andrew. *Eating Well for Optimum Health*. New York:
  Alfred A. Knopf, 2000.

About the Author

Karen Haywood is an editor and freelance writer. She has written nonfiction books for students on topics such as the state of Georgia, endangered animals, and human anatomy and physiology.